The Food You Eat

George Ivanoff

Contents

What's For Lunch?

What do you have for lunch today? Let's look at the food in this lunchbox.

This lunch tastes good – and is good for you, too! It has all the things needed for a healthy meal.

Foods have different things in them that help you grow and stay healthy. These things are called **nutrients**. It is important to eat different types of foods to get all the nutrients that your body needs.

When you eat lunch (or any other meal!), make sure you have plenty of foods from these groups:

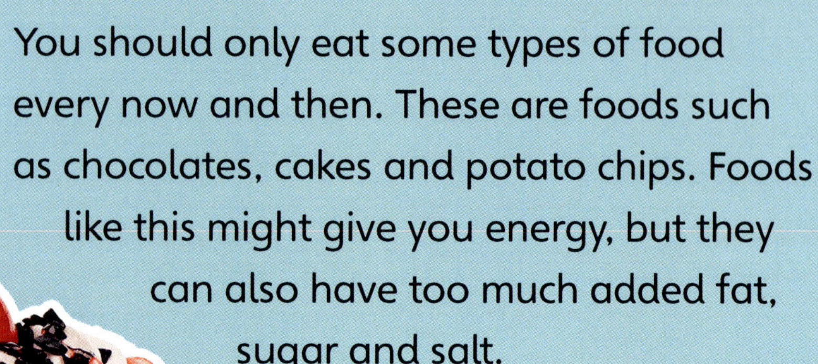

You should only eat some types of food every now and then. These are foods such as chocolates, cakes and potato chips. Foods like this might give you energy, but they can also have too much added fat, sugar and salt.

Next time you have lunch, think about the types of food you are eating.

Fruit and Vegetables

This lunch box has plenty of fruit and vegetables – an apple, an orange, carrot sticks, lettuce and tomato.

Jelly Gums

Did You Know?

A tomato is a fruit, not a vegetable! That's because it has seeds. Avocados, pumpkins and cucumbers are all fruit, too.

It is important to eat a variety of different fruit and vegetables because they each have different **vitamins** that your body needs.

IMPORTANT VITAMINS YOUR BODY NEEDS

Vitamin	Benefit	Found in
Vitamin A	is good for your eyesight	carrots spinach sweet potato cantaloupe dried apricots
B group vitamins	help keep your blood healthy	bananas avocados mushrooms sweet corn lima beans 
Vitamin C	helps your body fight disease	red capsicum broccoli oranges strawberries apples 
Vitamin E	keeps your skin healthy	olives cabbage pumpkin blackberries mangoes 
Vitamin K	helps your blood to clot (thicken) so that cuts and scratches stop bleeding	spinach lettuce broccoli blueberries

Most people get their fruit and vegetables from a market or supermarket. Do you know where they came from first?

Some people grow their own fruit and vegetables at home. Do you have a fruit tree or a vegetable patch in your garden?

Bread

The sandwich in this lunchbox is made with wholemeal bread. So, what is bread made from?

Bread is made from flour, and flour is made from grain.

Did You Know?

Different flours are made from different types of grain. The most common is wheat. There are also flours made from rye, maize, barley and oats.

Bread:
from the farm to your lunchbox

1 Farmers grow and harvest (cut down) the wheat, which is stored in large silos.

2 The wheat is taken to a flour mill where it is ground into flour.

3 Bakers use the flour to make bread.

4 You buy the bread at a bakery or a supermarket.

5 You eat the bread.

There are two types of bread – raised bread and flattened bread.

Raised bread is made with yeast. It is called leavened bread. The **yeast** is mixed with the flour before baking and makes the bread light and fluffy.

Flat bread is made without yeast. It is called unleavened bread.

Did You Know?

Pita bread is unleavened bread.

Most people buy their bread from a shop. But you can also make your own. The main ingredients are flour, water, yeast and salt.

There are many different recipes for bread that add other ingredients, including milk, eggs and butter.

Do you want to have homemade bread for lunch? Here is a simple bread recipe that you can try.

Ingredients

- 310 millilitres of water
- 2 teaspoons of oil
- 1 teaspoon of salt
- 2 teaspoons of sugar
- 500 grams of flour
- 1½ teaspoons of dry instant yeast

Method

1. Mix all the ingredients in a bowl so it makes a dough.

2. Put the dough on a floured surface and knead for 10 minutes.

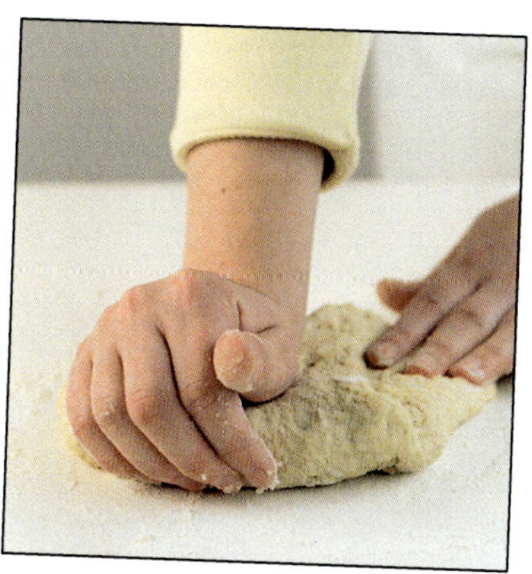

3. Let the dough rest for 20 minutes.

4. Knead the dough again for 5 minutes.

5. Put the dough into a baking tin.

6. Bake in an oven at 180 degrees Celsius for about 35 minutes.

If you don't like bread or sandwiches, there are a lot of other tasty things you can eat:

- rice paper rolls
- home-made sushi
- rice balls
- rice cakes
- pasta salad.

Fish and Eggs

There is tuna (fish) and egg in this lunchbox. These foods are good sources of **protein**. Your body needs protein to grow, heal and stay healthy.

Did You Know?

Fish is sometimes called "brain food". This is because it is a good source of Omega 3, a special group of fats, which your brain needs to work well.

Eggs are a good source of protein, and have lots of nutrients as well. Each one comes in its own, individually wrapped package, too!

How do you like your eggs?

- hard boiled
- scrambled
- fried
- poached
- baked
- in omelettes
- in frittatas
- in quiches.

Eggs: from the farm to your lunchbox

Some people keep chickens as pets so they can have fresh eggs every day.

What if you don't like fish or eggs? Here are some other foods you can eat for lunch that have a lot of protein:

- red meat, such as beef
- white meat, such as chicken
- nuts and seeds
- legumes/beans

Not everyone eats meat and fish. Many people are vegetarian. Vegetarians don't eat meat, chicken or fish. They need to get the nutrients found in meat and fish from other foods, such as tofu, nuts, seeds, legumes and beans.

Snack Attack!

Instead of having meat or fish at lunch time, pack a container of hummus (made from chickpeas) with carrot sticks or pita bread for dipping. This is a great vegetarian snack full of goodness!

Yoghurt and Cheese

This lunch box has yoghurt and cheese, which are both dairy products. Dairy products are foods made from milk.

Dairy products are an important source of calcium and protein. Calcium is really important to help you grow strong bones and healthy teeth.

Dairy products can be made from milk.

Milk comes from different animals, such as:

- cows
- sheep
- goats
- buffalo
- camels
- yaks.

Did You Know?

Western countries, such as Australia and Britain, mostly use cow's milk. India is the top user of buffalo milk.

Cheese is made by separating milk into two parts – the solid part, called curd; and the liquid, called whey. The curd is then pressed and turned into cheese.

Cheese: from the farm to your lunch box

1 Farmers keep cows and milk them.

2 The milk is taken to the dairy where it is made into cheese.

3 The cheese is taken to the supermarket and other food stores.

4 You buy the cheese.

Yoghurt is made by adding **bacteria** to milk. These bacteria help to thicken the milk into yoghurt.

Sweets

As well as the healthy food in the lunch box, there are some sweets – a small bag of Jelly Gums.

Many foods have sugar added to them. Adding sugar makes things sweeter, but it does not add any nutrients to help you have a healthy body. Sweets, such as lollies and chocolates, have a lot of added sugar.

Sweets may taste great, but they're not good for you. They're fine as a treat, but you should not eat too many of them.

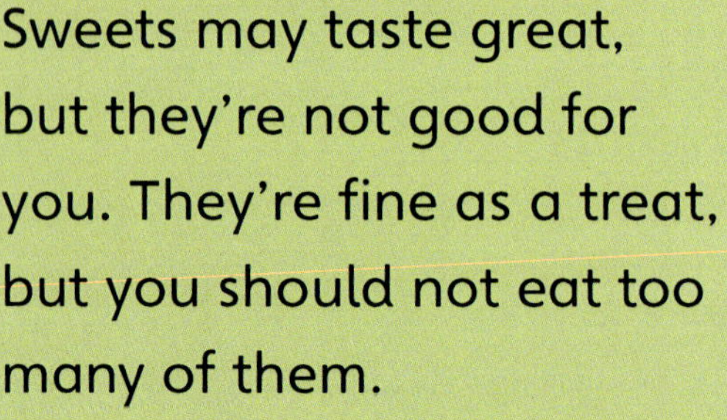

Some sweets are not as bad for you as others. A blueberry muffin gets most of its sweetness from the fruit rather than added sugar, so it is better for you than lollies, which have lots of added sugar.

Most sugar is made from a giant grass called sugarcane. The juice is squeezed from the cane, and everything other than the sugar is removed.

Lollies:
from the farm to your lunchbox

1 Farmers grow and harvest sugarcane.

2 The sugarcane is taken to the refinery and made into sugar.

3 The sugar is taken to a factory where it is made into lollies.

4 The lollies are taken to the supermarket and other food stores.

5 You buy the lollies.

The Food You Eat

Food is an important part of our lives. We need to eat in order to live. And we need to eat different types of foods to stay healthy.

Sometimes food can make people sick.

If this happens to you, it may mean you have an **allergy**. Some foods that can cause allergies are peanuts, eggs and milk.

Next time you eat something, think about what you are eating.

What's in your lunch today? Where does it come from?

Glossary

allergy	a dangerous response to a substance, such as a particular food
alternative	another way or possibility
bacteria	a microscopic organism
nutrients	the healthy parts of food that your body needs
protein	a nutrient that is in many foods
silo	a large storage container
vitamins	nutrients found in some foods that you need to grow and live
yeast	a type of fungus